Gabby's Special Dice

by Ariel Devoy

First Edition

ISBN 979-8-89297-042-6

95 Percent Group LLC

475 Half Day Road, Suite 350 • Lincolnshire, IL 60069

847-499-8200

95percentgroup.com

Printed in the United States of America.

10 9 8 7 6 5 4 3 2 1

R1.9.24

Table of Contents

Chapter 1

Wow, Cats Can Talk?!

Wow, Cats Can Talk?!

Initial Blends, Consonant Digraphs, Silent Letters, Complex Consonants

Initial blends

spot	Brad	flops
trap	frog	ground
snubs	class	black
class	clam	brush
brag	glum	front

Consonant digraphs

back	dashes	black
shade	rock	brush
push	picks	
luck	stick	

Silent letters

comb
knob

Complex consonants

budge
stretches

High-frequency words

Irregular

of	about
there	their
some	come
only	from
to	looks
your	says
want	would
what	

Challenge words

playground
school
Simon

In the back of the school playground, there is a spot of shade.

Some kids say that there is a trap there. A trap that you would only go to if you want to push your luck.

But Gabby snubs what other kids say. She likes to explore. So after the bell rings, she dashes out to the spot of shade.

She cannot wait to see
what she will find. She will go
back to class and brag about
what she finds.

She can't wait to tell Brad.
Brad found a frog.

The class loved that frog
so much, the frog is now their
class pet. She wants to find
something cool, like Brad did.

So Gabby looks and looks.
She finds a comb, a knob,
and a rock with a shape like a
clam. But there is nothing like
a frog.

Gabby begins to feel glum. She flops onto the ground and sighs.

She picks up a stick and
pokes the ground.

Then she sees something black come out from the brush. It is a black cat. The cat looks at her and stretches.

"Hello," the cat says.

Gabby gasps and holds the stick in front of her.

The cat does not budge.

"My name is Simon," the cat says.

Chapter 2

Making a Deal

Making a Deal

Long Vowel Silent-e, Open Syllables, Hard and Soft c/g

Long vowel silent-e

gracefully	slide	cake
smiles	like	trade
pace	home	shiny
price	races	nice
gripes	bake	dice

Open syllables

be
she

Hard and soft c/g

gracefully	races
pace	nice
price	
sagely	

High-frequency words

Regular

saw	will	
his	for	
has	now	
can		
it		
this		

Irregular

were
have
does
give
are
always

Challenge words

money
Tío
Angel
parents
front
picture

"Simon?" Gabby asks.

"Yes, I am Simon the Magic Cat." Simon stretches gracefully. "I saw you were feeling glum. I can help."

Gabby smiles. "I want to find the best thing ever!"

Simon begins to pace and wag his tail.

"Yes, it would be great to find the best thing ever," he says. "I can give you that, but it has a price."

"A price?" Gabby gripes. "I don't have money."

"A price does not always mean money." Simon jumps to the top of the playground slide.

"If you give me something
you used to like, I can give you
something everyone will like."

Gabby taps her chin.
"Okay. I will go home to get it."

Simon nods sagely. "This will not be a waste."

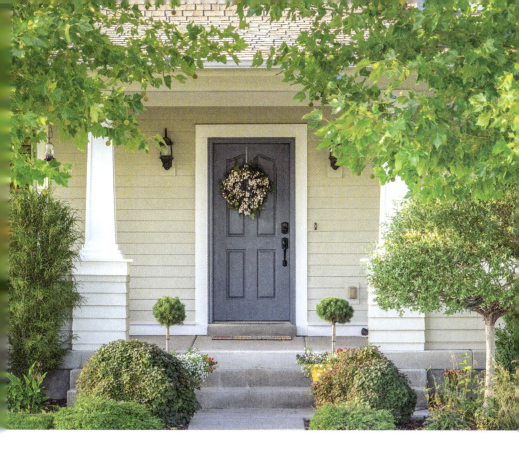

Gabby races home and looks for something to give to Simon.

"Gabby! Welcome home!
Do you want to help us bake
Tío Angel's cake?" Gabby's
parents ask her.

"No, *mamá*. I am looking
for something I used to like to
trade for something everyone
will like."

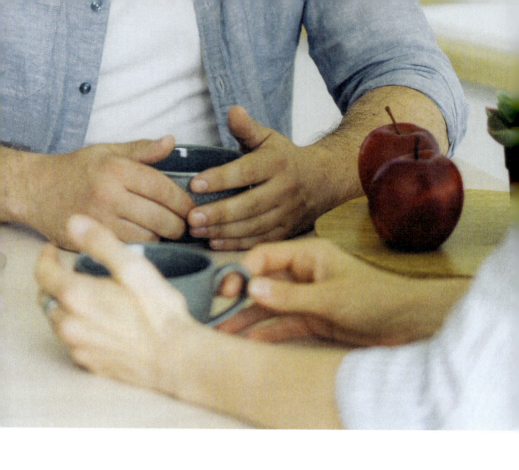

Mama and Papa look sad.

"Okay, Gabby. But remember, something shiny and nice is not always better than what you have now."

Gabby nods as Mama and Papa leave. She looks at a picture of *Tío* Angel. In front of the picture are some dice.

Gabby grabs the dice and
runs back to the playground.

Chapter 3

The Rocketship

The Rocketship

Predictable and Unpredictable Vowel Teams

Predictable vowel teams

paws
right
fight
play

Unpredictable vowel teams

played   clouds
tail   believe
train   leave
threw   new
died   real

High-frequency words

Irregular

have
puts
front
don't
looks
sure
comes

Challenge words

Simon   spaceship
together   pushes
belonged   buttons
Tío   sometimes
Angel
disappeared
anymore
prefer

"Simon! I have it!" Gabby yells. She puts the dice in front of Simon.

Simon grabs the dice with
his paws. He spins them and
stacks them and unstacks
them.

His tail wags as he kicks and
knocks the dice together.

"I like them. Why don't you like them?" he asks.

Gabby looks at the dice.
"They belonged to my *Tío*
Angel. We played games on
the train together."

"We threw dice to see who
was right in a fight. But then
he disappeared."

"Mama and Papa said he died. So I don't play with the dice anymore."

Simon plays with the dice. "Are you sure you will prefer what I have over what you have?"

Gabby nods.

Simon jumps into the
shade and brings out a toy
spaceship with red flames.
Gabby pushes the buttons on
the side.

The spaceship comes to
life and spits thick clouds
of white smoke! It even has
straps!

Gabby straps and
re-straps the spaceship to her
back. She cannot believe it!

This will be all the rage in her class! Even Brad will like this!

"Thank you, Simon!"

Gabby runs off.

Simon watches Gabby leave. "She does not know yet, but sometimes new things become a real drag."

Chapter 4

I Miss You, *Tío* Angel

I Miss You, *Tío* Angel
Vowel-r

Vowel-r

her	irked	covered
transform	answer	colorful
stars	bursts	
share	anymore	
cares	picture	

High-frequency words

Irregular

loves	everyone
into	one
again	talk
does	walk
answer	

Challenge words

spaceship
kingdom
anymore
appear
parents
picture
colorful

Gabby loves her new spaceship! She shows it to Brad and Chuck and Chip and Chap.

She can transform the
room into a kingdom of stars.

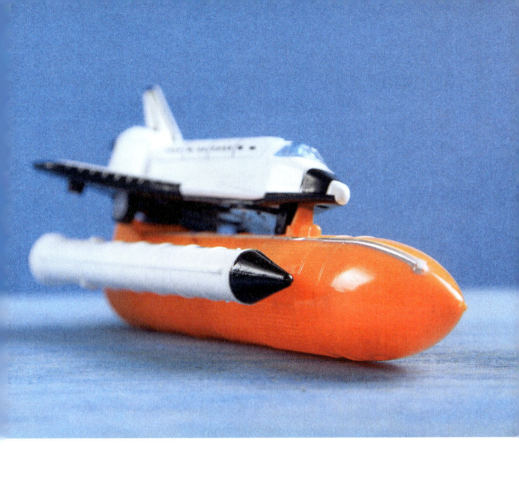

Everyone wants to share
the spaceship. Gabby loves
the fame.

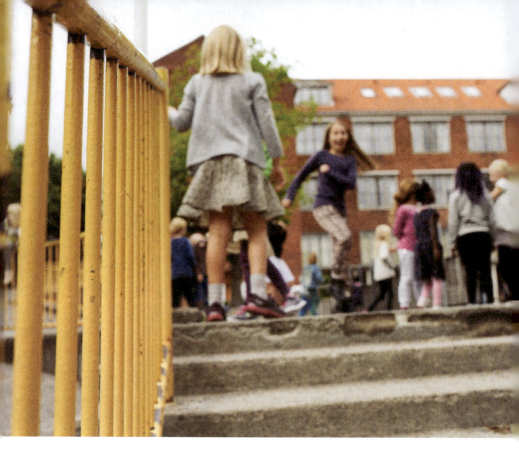

One day, Gabby brings her spaceship and no one cares anymore.

Not even Brad wants to
play with it! Gabby is irked.
She goes to find Simon.

"Simon! No one likes my spaceship anymore!" Gabby calls.

Simon does not appear.
"Simon!" Gabby calls again.

Simon does not answer.

Gabby heads home and bursts into tears.

"Gabby, what's wrong?" her parents ask.

"I traded *Tío* Angel's dice
for this new toy. Everyone
liked it, but now no one wants
to play with it. I don't want it
anymore!"

Mama and Papa hug
Gabby. "Do you want to talk
to *Tío* Angel?" they ask.

Gabby nods.

They walk to *Tío* Angel's picture, covered with colorful art of skulls and flowers.

"Today is *Dia de los Muertos,* Day of the Dead. He will be able to hear you today, Gabriela."

Gabby sits in front of *Tío*
Angel's picture. "*Tío*, I think I
did something wrong. I traded
your dice for a new toy."

"At first, everyone liked my new toy. But now no one likes it, not even me. I miss you. What do I do?"

Gabby closes her eyes. She sees *Tío* Angel on the train, when he gave her his dice. She feels her heart grow big.

Then Gabby thinks of the spaceship. She likes it, but she does not feel her heart grow big.

She opens her eyes. Her
spaceship is next to her.

The spot that used to hold the dice is empty. Gabby's heart hurts a bit.

"I miss my *Tío*. I need to get his dice back."

Chapter 5

A Meaningful Exchange

A Meaningful Exchange

Cumulative Review

Review of all phonics foci

arm	her	paw
you	mean	warm
twirls	grown	
tail	me	

High-frequency words

Regular

under
everything

Irregular

toward
walks
front
learned
something
what
anymore

Challenge words

value
rolls
happy
inside
head
meows
understand

Gabby walks toward
Simon. She holds her
spaceship under her arm.

Simon sits and waits for her. His black fur shines. "Did you like your spaceship, Gabby?" Simon asks.

Gabby nods. She places
the toy in front of Simon. "I
did. But I learned something."

Simon twirls his tail.
"What was it?"

Gabby sits in the dirt and looks at the spaceship. It is still a fun toy.

But it does not mean the
same to her as the pair of
dice did.

"I learned that new things
are nice, but it does not mean
as much as something that
has grown with me."

Simon lifts his paw. Under
it are the dice. "Everything
has a price. Not everything
has value."

Gabby reaches out and takes the dice. She looks at the dice and rolls them in her hands.

She feels happy and warm
inside. "Thank you, Simon."
Gabby says. She pets his
head.

Simon purrs and meows. Gabby cannot understand him anymore. Simon nudges the spaceship back to her.

Gabby smiles and takes the spaceship and the dice home.

Ariel Devoy is a writer, nature-lover, and cat-hugger. Ariel loved writing when she was in high school, but was unsure of her path, and went to college to learn Chinese and business management. She traveled the world and began sharing her experiences in her writing again! Now, she makes her stories from a little townhouse in a town that is nicknamed "The Center of the Universe," Ashland, Virginia.

Storyshares is focused on supporting older striving readers by creating a new shelf in the library specifically for them. The ever-growing collection features content that is compelling and culturally relevant for older students, teens, and adults, yet still readable at a range of lower reading levels.

Storyshares generates content by engaging deeply with writers, bringing together a community to create this new kind of book. With more intriguing and approachable stories to choose from, striving readers are improving their skills and beginning to discover the joy of reading. For more information, visit storyshares.org.

Easy to Read. Hard to Put Down.